BUXTON

Text by Louise Maskill

Walks by Mark Titterton

INTRODUCTION

One thousand feet above sea level and situated on the River Wye, the Derbyshire spa town of Buxton has been an important centre for trade and tourism for centuries. The area has been inhabited since Mesolithic times, and the Romans knew the settlement as Aquae Arnemetiae – the waters of the goddess of the grove – and made votive offerings of coins which were found during excavations of the town's Roman wells and baths. The town's name was first recorded as Bucstones around 1100, with the area renowned for its holy wells throughout the medieval period. Mary Queen of Scots is known to have visited in the sixteenth century to take the waters during her long period of captivity at the hands of Elizabeth I.

ABOVE: Solomon's Temple – Buxton Country Park

Buxton began to attract the nobility in the seventeenth century, benefiting from the fashion for treatment with curative waters and boosted by investment from successive Dukes of Devonshire. However, the town's most significant period of development dated from 1840 to 1910, spanning a busy period of Victorian industry and tourism when visitors were drawn by the health-giving thermal and cold springs as well as the natural beauty of the surrounding Peak District.

Health tourists stayed at the town's growing collection of hydropathic hotels and took treatments in the natural and thermal baths, with options ranging from Turkish and Russian baths to steam baths, douches and hot and cold plunge pools. The arrival of the railways in 1863 brought excursionists from Manchester and further afield, and the town's popularity grew; at its height Buxton was playing host to some four thousand visitors per week.

Hydropathic treatments became less fashionable in the early twentieth century, when the First World War changed the social scene forever. However, Buxton's decline as a health resort was counterbalanced by a rise in its importance as a local cultural centre and by the growing popularity of outdoor activities. The Peak District National Park was created in 1951, bringing renewed trade in tourism, and the Buxton Festival was inaugurated in 1979, injecting new life into the Opera House and ensuring Buxton's place in the national and international calendar of celebrations of opera, music and literature. Today Buxton is a vibrant centre for visitors and locals alike; this book will introduce you to the history and attractions of this fascinating town, and guide you as you explore the local environs.

ABOVE: The Pump Room at St Ann's Well provided thermal water for drinking
OPPOSITE PAGE TOP: The Old Hall Hotel   BOTTOM: The Slopes

THE OLD HALL AND THE SLOPES

The Old Hall Hotel was originally built by George Talbot, Sixth Earl of Shrewsbury (and fourth husband of the redoubtable Bess of Hardwick) in 1573 to provide a safe house for the imprisoned Mary Queen of Scots, who loved Buxton and visited the town regularly to receive treatment for rheumatism. The hall was later enlarged and reconstructed by the Second Duke of Devonshire; the present façade dates from the 1670s, but the older building (a four-storey tower) remains within and behind. The hotel is reputed to be the oldest in England.

The Slopes (also known as St Ann's Cliff) face the Crescent across a wide forecourt, and form a landscaped series of terraced walks, originally laid out about 1818 but extensively remodelled in the 1840s by Sir Joseph Paxton, who was head gardener to the Sixth Duke of Devonshire at Chatsworth. The undulating paths provided a range of challenging walks of different gradients for the recovering invalid, and were an integral part of the water cures offered by Buxton's spas and hydros.

THE CRESCENT, THE DEVONSHIRE ROYAL HOSPITAL AND THE DEVONSHIRE DOME

Buxton's famous Crescent was designed by the architect John Carr and financed by the Fifth Duke of Devonshire between 1780 and 1784. It was intended to transform lowly Buxton into a fashionable spa resort to rival others like Bath, Tunbridge Wells and Matlock Bath, and the sweeping Georgian architecture certainly lends an air of elegance. Over the centuries it has housed hotels, lodging houses, a ballroom, shops, council offices and a library. The long-overdue redevelopment of the Crescent was completed 2020. It is now a prestigious spa hotel complex.

The Great Stables were completed by 1789 to service the Crescent, but the building was soon converted to serve the growing invalid population; by 1881 it had been fully converted into the Devonshire Royal Hospital, with its crowning glory of the Devonshire Dome. This architectural marvel covers just over half an acre with a diameter of over 150 feet – larger than any of the domes at the Pantheon, St Peter's in Rome and St Paul's in London, and at the time of construction it was the largest unsupported dome in the world. The hospital finally closed in 2000 (one of the last hydropathic hospitals to do so), and the building now houses the Buxton & Leek College and a restaurant, a café, beauty and spa salons, as well as providing a stunning venue for weddings, banquets and other events.

TOP LEFT: The Devonshire Dome   TOP RIGHT: The Crescent

THE PALACE HOTEL, ST ANNE'S CHURCH AND THE CHURCH OF ST JOHN THE BAPTIST

Travel to Buxton in the nineteenth century was mainly by coach or cart along turnpike roads, which were maintained by the Devonshire Estate. However, rail travel arrived in the centre of Buxton in 1863, with separate stations built to service two competing railway companies and provide services south east to Matlock and north east to Whaley Bridge and onwards to Manchester.

With the new influx of tourists came the need for more accommodation; the Palace Hotel was originally known as the Buxton Hotel, and was intentionally sited near the two railway stations. It changed hands in 1867 after the original investors got into financial difficulties; the new shareholders included the Seventh Duke of Devonshire and local businessmen, the rebranded Palace Hotel became prosperous and popular.

The Parish Church of St John the Baptist was the Fifth Duke of Devonshire's final gift to the town; he died in 1811 after commissioning the church, which was dedicated in 1812. It is a spacious and welcoming church in a central location opposite the Devonshire Dome and near the Opera House; indeed, it is sought after as a venue for the arts, particularly during the Buxton International Festival in July each year. Other places of worship in the town include St Anne's Catholic Church on Terrace Road, and the oldest public building in Buxton – a small church at the top of Bath Road also dedicated to St Anne.

TOP: The Palace Hotel BOTTOM: Church of St John the Baptist, St John's Road

THE TOWN BATHS, THE PUMP ROOM, ST ANN'S WELL AND BUXTON'S WELL DRESSING

The town's Natural and Thermal Baths were in the Crescent, opened in 1854 near the site of the original Roman baths. The treatment facilities were open to genteel paying clients, but there were also charity baths for patients at the Devonshire Royal Hospital (these were later moved to George Street and the back of the Old Hall, to make more space for paying visitors in the Crescent). The Town Bath buildings (now the Cavendish Arcade-a selection of interesting individual retail outlets) feature the largest stained glass barrel-vaulted ceiling in Britain.

The Pump Rooms, providing thermal and iron-bearing (chalybeate) water for drinking, were originally situated in the Crescent but were later moved to the bottom of the Slopes. The Pump Room building now houses the Buxton Visitor Centre, where you will find plenty of useful information about the many year-round events in Buxton. At the same time take the opportunity to browse the shop which stocks a wide array of original gifts.

St Ann's Well harks back to the prehistory of the town, when medieval pilgrims and the Romans before them visited sacred shrines around the area's natural wells (although few traces of these early sites remain today). This public well was created to provide a free source of natural spring water for the townsfolk, as a condition of the Buxton Enclosures Act 1772; the well has stood at its present site, at the foot of the Slopes opposite the Crescent, since around 1780 when the Fifth Duke built the Crescent, although the current well building dates from 1940. Visitors can drink straight from the well or fill their bottles there with Buxton spa water, warm, straight from the source.

Derbyshire well dressings are a popular tradition, where the locals decorate public sources of water in the town to give thanks for the supply of free fresh water. Thought to date back to pagan times, the

ABOVE: St Anne's Well **OPPOSITE PAGE:** St Anne's Well Dressing

ST ANNE'S WELL / WELL DRESSING

practice was embraced by the Victorians and revived in Derbyshire during the nineteenth century; Buxton has decorated its three wells since 1842 when the Sixth Duke of Devonshire provided piped water to the town and the wells were dressed to give thanks.

The first modern well dressing in Buxton may have been dedicated to the Cavendish family rather than to God, but the practice continues with colourful displays made of flowers, seeds and leaves placed at the town's wells over a week in July each year. The well dressing queen is crowned, the funfair arrives, and the whole town celebrates Carnival Day at the end of well dressing week. This is a tradition not to be missed!

THE SQUARE, BUXTON MUSEUM AND ART GALLERY, AND SPRING GARDENS

The Square, opposite the Opera House and the Pavilion Gardens, was completed in 1806, built by the Fifth Duke of Devonshire as part of the first major period of investment in the town. The development was originally conceived as a group of lodging houses, but over the years it has housed shops, cafés, medical consulting establishments and boarding houses.

Buxton Museum and Art Gallery, on Terrace Road, houses geological and archaeological collections, fine art and photographic archives, complemented by a busy programme of temporary exhibitions throughout the year. Spring Gardens has always been a commercial area and was developed as a shopping street by the Victorians, with elegant cast iron and glass colonnades and a small well, one of the three dressed during the town's well dressing in July each year. The street still forms the main shopping area of the town, housing the Springs indoor shopping centre and encompassing the old Royal Hotel building, probably the earliest Victorian building of note, completed in 1852 and built to complement the Crescent.

TOP LEFT: The Square
RIGHT: The Boyd Dawkins Room at Buxton Museum and Art Gallery

THE PAVILION GARDENS

Overlooked by the Broad Walk, a fashionable Victorian terrace, the Pavilion Gardens were laid out on land donated by the Seventh Duke of Devonshire, originally designed by Sir Joseph Paxton and developed by Edward Milner in the 1870s into gardens, serpentine walks, streams and a lake. Paxton's influence is clearly seen in the glass and iron pavilion, reminiscent of the Crystal Palace in London also designed by Paxton, which was built to provide a venue for concerts by the town's band (paid for by the Duke) and for promenading in wet weather.

The gardens opened in 1871 and met with instant success – so much so that their popularity led to overcrowding and the need for extension. The Concert Hall opened in 1876, along with a roller skating rink in the park (which was flooded and used for ice skating in the winter).Later additions included the Pavilion Theatre in 1889. The whole complex has recently undergone a stylish and sympathetic restoration to provide space for a cinema, cafés, the Buxton Brewery Bar, and a gift boutique encompassing "The Gallery in the Gardens"-which is an art gallery, featuring work by local artists and artisans.

TOP: Broad Walk MIDDLE: Boating on the Lake
BOTTOM: The Concert Hall (now known as the Octagon) in the Pavilion Gardens

THE CONCERT HALL, CONSERVATORY, OPERA HOUSE AND BUXTON INTERNATIONAL FESTIVAL

Buxton Concert Hall, now known as the Octagon, was designed by Buxton architect Robert Rippon Duke and built during the expansion and development of the Pavilion Gardens in the mid-1870s. With its stunning dome it has played host to band concerts, fairs, dances, markets and fêtes. Unfortunately it has been closed for repairs but is scheduled to re open at the end of 2018. The Conservatory, at the side of Buxton Opera House, is a peaceful environment filled with plants and palms from around the world, offering a tranquil space to wander and enjoy the scents of the flowers. Don't miss the little pond with its goldfish.

The Opera House itself, situated in the Square, was designed by Frank Matcham (who also designed the Palladium and the Coliseum in London) as a new theatre for the town and a grand entrance to the Pavilion Gardens. It opened in 1903 and was used extensively for live performances until 1927, and then as a cinema. Falling attendance led to its eventual closure in 1976, but after a short period of dereliction it was restored and reopened in 1979, now seating just over nine hundred people. The addition of an orchestra pit to the otherwise unaltered Matcham design has meant that it is well able to host the annual Buxton International Festival in July each year, a prestigious international celebration of opera with a reputation for staging rarely performed works. The theatre hosts a wide variety of shows (including stand up, musicals, classical concerts, drama, ballet and dance) almost every night of the year and tours of the theatre are now offered. Details to be found in their programme and on the website.

The Festival's original concentration on opera has expanded to encompass other music and literature, as well as the Buxton Fringe an open-access arts event which runs concurrently with the Festival. The Fringe stages dance, drama, music, poetry, comedy, films and exhibitions, and together with the main Festival it attracts the highest quality of performers and artists, ensuring that the town of Buxton truly comes alive throughout the month of July.

THE OPERA HOUSE

TOP: Buxton Opera House and (*below*) the auditorium

OPPOSITE PAGE: The Conservatory in the Pavilion Gardens

Walk 1 – Buxton Country Park and Solomon's Temple

Length: 3¾ miles / 6 km (approx. 1 hour 30 mins)

Terrain: Paths, road/pavement, some steep woodland sections and stiles. Optional steps up Solomon's Temple (and within Poole's Cavern, if you choose to visit)

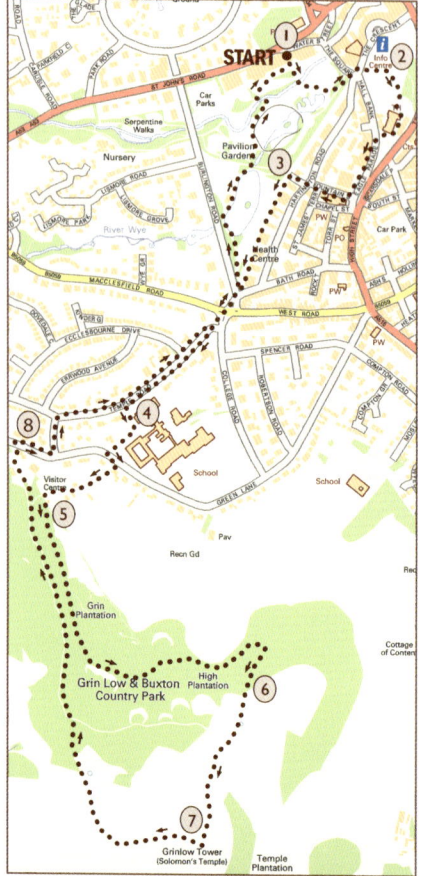

This walk will take you on a circular loop from the Pavilion Gardens and up through Higher Buxton to Poole's Cavern, Grinlow Woods and Buxton Country Park, taking in the fine views from the top of Solomon's Temple, a fortified hilltop folly funded by public subscription and built in the nineteenth century to provide work for the local unemployed.

In the seventeenth and eighteenth centuries Grinlow Woods were the site of extensive lime workings, as evidenced by the hollows and mounds found throughout the woods which were once the kilns and dwellings of the lime workers and their families. However, the industrial landscape did not please everyone, and the Sixth Duke of Devonshire planted Grinlow Woods in the 1820s to hide the eyesore. The area is now a site of special scientific interest due to the rich plant, animal and insect life which thrives here.

Poole's Cavern, which you pass twice on this walk, is well worth a visit. It is open daily throughout the year, and offers regular tours of the stunning showcave as well as a gift shop and café. Allow an extra couple of hours if you would like to include a visit to the cave on your walk.

1. From the entrance to the Pavilion Tea Rooms (in the Pavilion Gardens), walk down the steps straight ahead to cross a wide footbridge over the river. Turn left towards the opposite corner of the gardens to pass through a wrought iron gate. Cross straight over the road to the Old Hall Hotel, turn right, and then cross another road by the corner of the hotel and head up the short flight of steps leading to the Slopes. Continue up towards the distinctive War Memorial on your left.

2. From the War Memorial continue on the footpath along an avenue of trees to the entrance of Buxton Town Hall. Turn left then immediately right to walk around to the front of the building and to the Market Cross. From here walk across to the pavement on the right. Just beyond Sainsburys take the next turn on the right into Fountain Street. Walk down the pavement all the way to Broad Walk, crossing a junction half way down as you go.

3. Turn left along Broad Walk, continue to the end and cross over Burlington Road. Then bear left towards the junction with Macclesfield Road and make your way to a pedestrian crossing with traffic lights. Go over the Macclesfield Road here and walk up Temple Road. Passing the entrance of the Buxton Medical Practice on your right. Cross to the pavement on the opposite side of the road. You will shortly pass the entrance to Buxton Community School. Take the next footpath on the left adjacent to some metal railings. **Note:** there is no footpath signpost here, so be careful not to miss the turn.

4. Follow the footpath around the perimeter of the school to eventually join another road. Cross straight over the road and turn left, and then after a few yards turn right down a track which will bring you to the car park for Poole's Cavern. Bear left around the edge of the car park to some steps and a footpath into Woods.

5. Turn almost immediately left after going through a gate onto the lower footpath. You will pass a large and impressive wood carving depicting local wildlife. After a few more metres stay left on a broad footpath and keep to the green waymarkers. At another fork in the path with some wooden steps ahead, stay to the left. At the next fork, stay on the main broader path which bears right and climbs uphill to a gate in a stone wall.

6. Go through the gate and follow the eroded footpath directly uphill. You will now catch your first glimpse of Solomon's Temple on the horizon ahead. Continue up to the tower and enjoy the views from the top before returning to the entrance doorway.

7. Go left out of the entrance and head towards the stone wall. Follow the line of the wall going downhill, and just before a stile bear right and walk across to another stile signed to Poole's Cavern. You are now back in Grinlow Woods.  Stay on this path all the way down through the woods, looking out for the larger-than-life sculpture of a miner as you go! Ignore some steps down to Poole's Cavern on your right, continuing ahead to pass a cottage on your left before joining the road at the bottom of the woods.

8. Turn right along the road, and after a short distance take the first left down Temple Road which bears sharp right after a short distance. At the Macclesfield Road go over the pedestrian crossing you passed earlier, and return to the Pavilion Gardens.

13

Walk 2 – Corbar Woods and Corbar Cross

Length: 2½ miles / 4 km (approx. 1 hour 15 mins)

Terrain: Paths, road/pavement, some steep woodland sections and stiles.

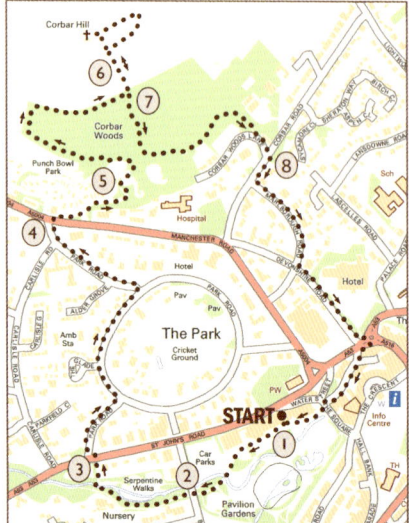

This walk takes you through Victorian landscaped gardens and a residential area with links to Vera Brittain, climbing through Corbar Woods and up to Corbar Cross, and then back down to the Pavilion Gardens passing the Devonshire Dome.

The Pavilion Gardens' Serpentine Walks extend along the River Wye at the western end of the park and were laid out by Joseph Paxton during the Sixth Duke's beautification of the town. The river flows over a series of smooth-stepped cascades and the surrounding parks and paths are calm and peaceful.

Vera Brittain, the author of Testament of Youth, lived in Buxton during her girlhood and served as a nurse here during the First World War before also serving in London, Malta and France. As well as writing prolifically she was a lifelong pacifist and campaigner. She died in 1970 and her ashes were scattered in Italy on the grave of her beloved brother Edward, who was killed in the First World War.

Corbar Woods is an area of ancient woodland which puts on stunning displays of bluebells in the spring, crowned by Corbar Cross above the woods on the summit of Corbar Hill. At 1433 feet above sea level this is a magnificent viewpoint – well worth the climb!

Finally, if you have time members of the public are allowed to enter the Devonshire Dome, where you can marvel at the architecture and the acoustics of this unique space, as well as visiting the café for some well-earned refreshments!

1. From the entrance to the Pavilion Tea Rooms (in the Pavilion Gardens), turn right towards the iconic Octagon building and continue part way along the side of the swimming and Fitness Centre (on your right). Prior to the car park, turn left on the footpath (signposted to Play Area) down to a footbridge over the river. Cross the bridge and continue straight ahead up the path to reach Burlington Road.

2. Cross straight over the road to a footpath on the left leading to the Serpentine Walks. There is an information panel at the entrance to the walks. Follow the path straight ahead with the river on your right to eventually cross a footbridge on the right, and then walk up to St Johns Road.

3. Cross straight over road and turn up Park Road almost opposite. Stay on the left side of the pavement as you walk uphill. At the junction turn left. You will shortly cross the entrance to Buxton Ambulance Station on your left. Take the next left turn, and then walk up the road to join the Manchester Road – but before you do, cross the junction to take a look at the Blue Plaque dedicated to Vera Brittain who lived in the house here from 1907 to 1914 (house not open to the public).

4. On reaching the junction with the Manchester Road, cross directly over to the pavement on the other side of the road and turn right. After a few yards take a footpath on the left by the bus stop which leads up into Corbar Woods.

5. Shortly after passing through a gate, where the path forks bear left and then right at the next fork, climbing all the while. At a green 'ring of trees' waymarker bear left onto a broader path, and then stay left and follow this path all the way to the top of the woods. The path eventually bends around to the right and follows the line of the wall (on your left); here you will catch your first glimpse of Corbar Cross on the horizon above. Continue to go over a stile in the wall on the left into the adjacent field.

6. From here you can walk directly up to Corbar Cross, ascending the ridge through a gap in the rocks, or for a more gentle ascent bear right after the next stile (in front of the rocks) and follow the track that doubles back up to the ridge.

7. Return to the stile at the edge of the woods and take the footpath down through the woods. At a junction with another path turn left, and after about 20 metres go left again at another green waymarker. Follow the waymarked path to join a private lane, and then turn left and walk down to the road.

8. Turn right at the road. Take the next left turn into Marlborough Road, and at the next crossroads turn left and walk down Devonshire Road, passing the entrance to the Devonshire Dome on the way. At the bottom cross straight over the main road, and then bear right and turn left into George Street and continue towards the Opera House, and the Pavilion Gardens.

BUXTON SOUVENIR & GUIDE

FACT FILE

The Buxton Visitor Centre is located within the Pump Room, facing the Crescent (postcode SK17 6BH), and is fully accessible to less mobile visitors or those with disabilities.

The centre is open daily from 10am to 4.00pm in the summer, reduced opening hours in the Winter.
Please check the website for the latest opening hours - www.buxtoncrescentexperience.com/pump-room/
Telephone: 01298 214557   **email:** visitorinformation@buxtoncrescenttrust.org

The official website for the Peak District is www.visitpeakdistrict.com, and there is a wealth of other information about Buxton at www.visitbuxton.co.uk.

Poole's Cavern, a short walk from the centre, (see Walk 1) is a magnificent example of a Derbyshire limestone cave and should not be missed. Guided tours daily. Other attractions in the local area include a variety of show caves in Castleton, walking in the Peak District National Park, Goyt Valley, and the Staffordshire Moorlands. Don't miss the splendours of Chatsworth House and Haddon Hall, and a wide variety of outdoor activities at Carsington Water and other centres. Details of all these attractions and many more are available from the Tourist Information Centre in Buxton. Do also pick up your free copy of the Buxton Town Guide.

Published by Bradwell Books
9 Orgreave Close Sheffield S13 9NP
books@bradwellbooks.co.uk

The rights of Louise Maskill and Mark Titterton as authors of this work have been asserted by them in accordance with the Copyright, Design and Patents Act, 1988.

All rights reserved. No part of this publication may be reproduced, stored in a retrieval system or transmitted in any form or by any means, electronic, mechanical, photocopying, recording or otherwise without the prior permission of Bradwell Books.

British Library Cataloguing in Publication Data: a catalogue record for this book is available from the British Library.

2nd Revised Edition
ISBN: 9781910551981

Design by: Mark Titterton
Text by: Louise Maskill
Walks by: Mark Titterton
Typesetting and mapping: Mark Titterton
Photography: Mark Titterton
Print: Hobbs the Printers Ltd, Totton, Hants
Credits
Additional Photographs: Courtesy of Buxton Museum & Art Gallery p.8 (*right*). Poole's Cavern p. 12 – R. Shone
Maps: Contain Ordnance Survey data
© Crown copyright and database right 2017

> The information in this book has been produced in good faith and is intended as a general guide. Although the maps in this book are based on original Ordnance Survey mapping, walkers are always advised to use a detailed OS map.
>
> Bradwell Books and the authors have made all reasonable efforts to ensure that the details are correct at the time of publication. Bradwell Books and the authors cannot accept responsibility for any changes that have taken place subsequent to the book being published.
>
> It is the responsibility of individuals undertaking any of the walks listed in this book to exercise due care and consideration for their own health and wellbeing and that of others in their party. The walks in this book are not especially strenuous, but individuals taking part should ensure they are fit and well before setting off.

This book is an invitation to connect more fully with parts of yourself, with others and with the natural world, through the intimacy of a hand-written letter.

A Letter of Love.

Writing in this way allows us to travel along the avenues of our imagination. Opening up to our wisest, kindest Self; listening to the wisdom we all carry within.

In therapeutic settings, much attention is given to the importance of emotional regulation. It is my observation that writing letters in this way – letters grounded in compassion for others and Self – can help create an immensely powerful framework for understanding the breadth and depth of our emotional landscape. Informing the way we relate to ourselves, to others and to the world around us. Which in turn helps us create that sense of balance, or regulation, that so many of us are looking for.

To support this practice, you'll see that this book is filled with prompts and space to write letters *to*... as well as *from* – a chance to step out of your own shoes and into another's.

This practice of intentional, compassion-based writing enables us to express our innermost thoughts and feelings in ways that may not have felt available, allowable or achievable before.

The unifying factor is that each letter is written with love. Though, of course (and as we'll explore later), that can mean different things.

The *power* of the *unsent* letter

How to *use* this *journal*

You can use this journal in whatever way works best for you. There is no right way. There is no wrong way. Trust your heart, your wisdom and your pen. You may enjoy following these four steps:

However and wherever you decide to explore this Work, it can be useful to take time to hone your connection with the subject of your letter. I'll share more on ways that can help you do that later.

You may also find it useful to reflect on what comes up. Journaling further on key themes or sharing thoughts with a trusted other (being discerning about who and how you share). Often in life we are quick to move on from things, so allowing space for this kind of compassionate, deeper reflection may be a useful part of your process.

And... if there's a letter you simply don't want to write, that's okay.

Noticing the resistance and honouring it – not trying to effortfully break through it – can be a useful part of this practice.

Instead, be mindful of what emotions, assumptions, expectations, memories and beliefs are activated by it. Honour them. Give them and yourself whatever attention is needed.

Maybe one day you'll return to it.

Maybe not.

Either is, of course, okay.

Before writing, setting an intention can be a wonderful way of softening into what is asking to be written; deepening your connection with your wise, loving Self. This can be particularly useful if you notice any resistance rising up within you.

An intention is a positive statement in the present tense, stated three times, as though it is already happening. It often begins with I am. Some inspiration could be:

- I am ready to write from my heart
- I write these words in service of the highest good
- I hold myself and these words with deep compassion
- I open my heart to see the meaning within
- I ask love to be with me as I write

Maybe there's an intention that calls to you?

Connecting & *reflecting* with *love*

Writing my first Letter of Love (the one that led to all the others) was like landing and taking flight simultaneously. I felt deeply grounded, while the words flowed up and out.

There was something about the balance of freedom (to write whatever came) and the direction (of the prompt) that helped me release my resistance and uncertainty. The awareness of the importance of this balance led me to embrace the style of writing that I've come to call Flow Journaling.

Using compassion-based prompts, Flow Journaling is a way of tapping into our subconscious, enabling free-flow expression. Nothing is off limits. And there are no rules. This open-hearted, open-minded approach enables us to explore feelings, thoughts, beliefs, behaviours and experiences from fresh perspectives – helping us develop personal insight and grow.

I invite you to experiment with this approach here.

Writing these letters, you don't know what will come – part of this practice is learning not to be afraid of your own thoughts and feelings. Learning to trust, holding yourself, your words and the one you're writing to (or from) with love.

Of course, one of the curious aspects of writing the letters in this book is that they remain unsent.

The value of that may seem puzzling. Or perhaps powerful? Perhaps purposeful? Perhaps all three.

There are times in all our lives when something important remains unsaid. We know or sense or fear that saying it may not serve us, or the one we're thinking of. There can also be times when we wish we could speak the truth we hold within but simply can't see how. Or when something catches our inner eye and words want to form but sharing them seems too big, too small, too heavy, too ridiculous, too hard.

This is very much the power of the unsent letter.

Allow yourself the space – and licence – to say what needs to be said, without preconceptions of how it might be received. This releases constraints on communication. Constraints you may not have even fully known were there.

And.

Each of these letters is grounded in love.

This doesn't mean a rose-tinted, pretending-all-is-well kind of love. It is a deep love, coming from the source that, I believe, is within us all.

It feels important to add that there's a tenderness to putting pen to paper and holding the one we're writing to in our hearts. It seems it can (often, maybe, sometimes) bring forth a subtle quality to our words. As though we're forming a bridge between us and them. A pathway for the energy to flow.

And when we write from our belly or from deep within our heart (or wherever your Wisdom Self resides), with the clear intention of serving the highest good, we can find these pathways lead to wisdom, healing, clarity. They can at times feel utterly surprising or remind us of something that, deep down, we always knew.

Lastly, the Unsent Letter allows us to return to what we've written. At times, a useful practice in its own right. A chance to see how far we've come, what has changed – or what remains the same.

Always without judgement.

Simply with the curiosity of what now could be asking for your attention.

1 Create your space:
Find a comfortable place, free from distractions, and attend generously to all your senses – sight, sound, scent, taste, touch. A private space, essential oils, a beautiful view, devices on silent, peaceful music, a warm drink, candles, a blanket – these can all help give you what you need in the moment.

2 Set your intention:
Pause. Take a breath (or three), then place your hand on your heart. Notice any feelings or sensations – listen without judgement. Let yourself know it's safe to settle. And state your intention, in your mind or out loud, three times. Giving meaning to each word.

3 Choose your Letter of Love: Perhaps open a page at random. Or work through from the beginning – or follow a section at a time, trusting the order and flow. Maybe choose one prompt and write to it many times – it's something I love to do. The one you choose will be right for you.

4 Write: There are no rules here. Let the words form themselves as they spill from the end of your pen onto the page. Be free. This way of writing helps us tap into our deepest wisdom. It gently breaks down barriers that may have formed within us, releasing us to express our wisest truth.

To or *from?*

I mentioned before that the prompts in this journal include letters to... and letters from.

These letters can feel like very different things.

When we're writing to... we're writing from our own lived experience. We're building on the evidence (perceived or real) we have gathered and we're expressing what we believe to be ours to say.

When we're writing from... we're stepping into another's shoes. We're tapping into our empathy; our ability to put aside our OWN experience and feel into what it might be like for the one we are writing from.

This kind of writing can feel challenging. Depending on our life experience, accessing and developing our sense of another's thoughts and feelings may feel more or less available to us. And that's okay. The invitation is simply to experiment.

Maya Angelou, in all her wisdom, once commented: 'I think we all have empathy. We may not have enough courage to display it.' Having been seen as a fixed asset (you either had it or not), modern research now shows us that empathy is something we can all develop.

My own sense is that writing any of these letters can be a practice in courageously displaying empathy – as well as a practice in compassion and gratitude and releasing what no longer serves us.

As you explore the prompts that follow, you'll see they're broadly clustered. Each section follows an arc that travels from Self, out to Body, then widens out to Earth before drawing back in to Others and finally returning to Emotions.

For me, this arc feels a little like the practice of Metta, where we begin with Self before extending our loving kindness out to those we love, those with whom we have difficulty, and finally all beings… before returning back to Self. This can be a lovely meditation to use as part of your ritual of writing – I've recorded it for you here, if that feels useful.

You'll also see I share some of my own Letters of Love, as whole pieces or extracts. I was mindful as I wrote them that you would read them too, and so they may be a little different from when I write them just for me. But I've shared them in their rawness, just as they fell onto the page. Each one has given me an insight, and I'm grateful to them all. They are here in case they are useful for you too – either as you write in this book, or at another time.

innerworkproject.com/
product/letters-of-love

I have recorded a Metta meditation you can listen to here.

When things *feel a little* tricky

With some of the letter prompts, you may find you're holding old feelings that don't feel like love. Or perhaps it feels odd to write to a some*thing*, rather than a some*one*. Or you may notice the unfamiliarity of expressing love for a particular part of you.

That's all okay. (There are no rules, there are no rules, there are no rules.) Simply create your space, get settled, set your intention, write whatever arises… and see where it goes.

A technique that you may enjoy playing with could be to invite the kind, wise beings you are connected with to support you, as you write.

This could mean many things.

For some of us, it may be calling on the memory of a loving elder with whom we've felt a deep connection. For others, we may have a sense of the support of the Universe or a spiritual being with us. Or it might mean thinking of a dear friend or wise loved one.

Ultimately, this is YOUR practice. And you can approach it in WHATEVER way works well for you.

Playing, experimenting, exploring. Releasing any attachment to a learned belief of what's 'okay' and what's 'not okay'.

Sometimes I find the simplest approach of opening my journal and diving in feels right. At other times, I embrace the richness of ritual to support me.

The power of ritual comes from what we imbue into our actions. So, I might light a candle, meditate, drink cacao or draw an Angel Card before I begin. Perhaps using my intention to invite in the guidance I seek:

I ask my wise guide to be with me as I write.

Your ritual might look very different. The art is always remembering these are Letters of Love.

This willingness to practise compassion for others as well as compassion for all our parts, helps us create a sense of psychological safety, as we dig a little deeper beneath the surface of things. We learn to trust that in among our noisy mind, our wisest, kindest Self is always there.

It's important, too, to remember you only need to travel as far as feels okay for you. Trust your own process and allow what is asking to be written... with love.

Another technique I often use when I notice my own writing is slipping toward judgement or criticism, or feelings like shame or doubt, is to write: How can I bring more compassion here?

It is astonishing how much compassion we each hold within us, if we only ask it to speak. So, hold yourself gently if things feel a little tricky; respond with endless tenderness.

And if self-compassion feels hard to find, Dr Kristin Neff describes it as 'treating ourselves as we would a dear friend'. In other words, think about how you would most love to be writing... and write in that way.

Self

What comes up for you as you think of writing Letters of Love to your Self?

How is it to receive your own loving attention? Not simply – or only – as you are now, but as you were, as you might become?

So many of us have been trained out of paying this kind of deep, loving attention to ourselves. We learn that self-attention is selfish or that care of others must always overshadow care of ourselves. We learn these things because they can also be part of how we learned to fit in, to be a good citizen; to belong.

And yet.

These kinds of beliefs can obscure our view from what is also true:

That it is only when we are able to hold space for the whole of ourselves, for who we have been, who we are now and for the potential that's inside us, that we can also hold space for others in their wholeness too.

In these letters, we write to and from all versions of our Self: past, present and future. Switching perspective as we go.

This can feel hard. We are essentially the same core being in all our iterations, and yet, we can sometimes feel like a stranger to ourselves.

Research shows us one of the hardest things about ageing is that what lies ahead of us is an alien landscape, where our future Self is an unknown being. And so, putting steps into place that will eventually benefit this stranger (like: nutrition, savings, exercise, profound self-care) can feel so hard to action.

And.

One of the hardest things about reconciling with the past is that, as L. P. Hartley once wrote in *The Go-Between*, 'The past is a foreign country; they do things differently there.'

These SELF letters are a chance to greet all versions of yourself with love. To get to know yourself. To listen to the wisdom from before and beyond who you are today.

Maybe there are things you wished you knew 'then'? Maybe there are things you want to make sure you never forget? Maybe a conversation is needed between these different ages of you?

This is your *opportunity* to say it all. *With love.*

So this
fresh future
that opens up
before you is one
you can enter into
with a glad heart
and spring in your
step, because you
have a pocket full
of everything
you need to
greet it.

A letter of love from my future Self

A letter of love to my future Self

My love

I met you once.
Do you remember?

You were writing by the window of my stable. You had two people with you, helping manage all the wonderful books and talks and things that were arising out of the words that fell from your pen.

You looked so contented. Happy.

I think you were 83. It's very specific but that's how you appeared to me. It was such a relief to know I was going to become you. And made me want to know more about what might happen on the path to you – though I know that part of the marvellous thing of life is not 'needing to know', but trusting all will be well.

Anton was there too – he was pushing a wheelbarrow full of cut grass by the open door, so not much had changed there!

There are many years between me and you – how lucky I am to have all that time ahead. And I feel in my bones that you enjoyed them as much as I intend to. There was something so measured about the way you moved, as though you understood the true value of things – time, space, love – all the important things.

I want to say thank you too for the things you shared that day, and the messages I've heard whispered to me along the way.

I'm enjoying our life so thank you for helping me see that this could be true.

With love.

A letter of love to my younger Self

A letter of love from my younger Self

I see you. And I love you. I see you and I relish being with you. I see you and nothing about how you are today, tomorrow or in one thousand days could ever change the way I feel about you.

A letter of love from my wisest, kindest Self

A letter of love to my wisest, kindest Self

My dearest darling, wise and loving Self

Writing to you feels almost overwhelming. If you could see the smile on my face right now (which, of course, you can!), then you would know (which, of course, you do!) how delighted I am to be sitting here with you.

Your presence feels so strong within me right now. This energetic thrum of golden strings running through my limbs, my chest, my finger and toe tips, my face and neck and up out of my crown, only to pour down around me.

Blimey.

You are the light, the love, the wisdom, the kindness. It's you who's guided me. I cannot thank you enough.

There has been so much uncertainty along the way – and so much clarity. You, always there to balance things. To help me see that all I needed to do was settle deeper and listen fully. And now the energy has settled too, I feel as if the first part of this letter was written with a giddy joy – a missive from your biggest fan!

And now I sense you in me as a calm spirit, my system no longer

thrumming, purring gently like the Leo I am.

Thank you for all the words you've written through me.

Thank you for being there for me to turn to when – always when – I needed you.

Thank you for guiding me in any moment I'm unsure. I know I don't always listen straightaway, but I'm learning to more and more.

With love.

Body

One of my favourite practices when leading a retreat is to invite everyone present to speak from their Head, their Heart and their Hara (their wisdom or 'gut' instinct).

We do this by...

Closing our eyes, settling deeply with a meditation or a few nourishing breaths, before placing the fingertips of one hand lightly on the forehead and whispering: 'My head says...' And simply seeing what comes. Sometimes it takes a moment for something to come through. Sometimes it's an image, a feeling or words. It's all valid.

Then, we take a settling breath before placing one hand lightly on the heart, 'My heart says...' And again, we wait to see what we hear. Simply listening.

Then, another releasing breath, before placing a hand gently on the belly and whispering: 'My wisdom, or hara, says...'

Sometimes this is an open practice, where we are simply curious about whatever arises. Sometimes we're listening for the response to a particular question we've asked ourselves. The fascinating thing is how the answers change as we move down the body. The head is often very protective and fact-oriented, the heart is often softer and emotion-oriented, and the hara is often the one who really sees the deeper truth of the matter.

I invite you to try it now – either as an open enquiry, or in response to something you're seeking an answer to.

My Head says...
My Heart says...
My Hara or Wisdom says...

For so many of us, connecting with our bodies can feel highly complex. Thoughts of our physicality can raise a range of responses, especially if we've inherited or adopted stories about not being enough, or being too much.

If the following Letters of Love inspire you to do more, an extension to the prompts that follow could be to write to other parts of your body, perhaps in gratitude for how they've served you or to rebalance how you've thought of them in the past.

But, for now, these next few BODY letters are a deeper version of that Head, Heart, Hara practice. A beautiful place to begin this act of (re)connecting with your incredible body. With love.

Beautiful body

I sat by the fire the other evening and looked at your legs. My legs? Anyway, I realized the legs I was looking at – clad in my soft checked pyjamas – are the legs that have carried every single iteration of me. From when I first walked, to when I first ran for joy, to when I first stepped onto a dance floor, to every time I walk barefoot in the grass.

It astonished me. I'm still unsure quite why it felt so astonishing, but it was as if I could see all the ages of me in them. And it was so moving.

Did you notice how I held you? How I tucked your knees up tight and held you. How I lay your hands softly on your arms and knew them for what they are.

The same arms that wrapped around my mother's neck, that held my own child. And did you notice how I didn't wipe the tears that fell onto your cheeks; I let them tickle me, then dry where they fell.

And did you notice how your heart beat so hard as I saw and felt all this, and then settled into a soft, slow rhythm, so calm and comforting – I placed your hands over her, feeling each tiny thud within your ribs. Writing this makes me so glad to have found you.

I know you've always been here but for so so many many years I've not loved you as I could. I'm so so very very sorry for all that. And I'm so so very very glad you don't hold grudges and you just kept on holding me, holding me up, helping me hear, see, touch, taste and know all that is wonderful in the world.

With love.

A letter of love to my body

A letter of love to my heart

Tender heart

Thank you.

Thank you for opening.

Thank you for the pain I felt as you opened.

Thank you for helping me see how I had turned away from you, afraid of the enormity of what lay within.

Thank you for helping me see it's all the same. The joy and the pain. It all springs from you. Grief is not possible without you. Connection is not possible without you. Life itself is not possible without you.

Thank you for showing me how loving myself is the only pathway to loving others ever more deeply, and to being loved ever more deeply still.

With love.

Sweet child

Every time you place your hand on me, I know you are listening.

Every time you place your hand on me, I know you are listening.

Every time you place your hand on me, I know you are listening.

With love.

A letter of love from my heart

A letter of love to my head

A letter of love from my head

Listen. No need to push or pull. Just listen. No need to force or cling. Simply listen and you will hear the words that whisper within.

A letter of love from my hara (wisdom)

Earth

How do we begin to write to Earth?

How can we encompass her enormity, fragility, generosity and strength?

When I first saw the image of the pale blue dot, taken from hundreds of millions of miles away, I began to have a truer sense of the astonishing gift we have been given in this time and space: the land beneath our feet, the air in our lungs, the food and water in our bellies.

The sheer scale of the task of paying our deepest attention to the natural world can feel overwhelming at times. It can also be deeply inspiring, enlightening, moving – and it can certainly resize our own place in the Universe.

So, where do we start?

Curiosity may be our greatest ally here. As Albert Einstein noted,

'Look deep into nature, and then you will understand everything better.'

What a beautiful notion.

For me, it sparks a corresponding thought that everything in and on Earth comes from the same source. We can read that as Source – the Oneness, the Universe, the Everything, the All – or we can read it with our most pragmatic minds, with a small 's'. Meaning, of course the stuff of stars. You, me, us, them, they, it. We are, in a very profound sense, the same.

And so, we could see that looking deep into nature is a fundamental path to understanding ourselves.

I like this thought.

It helps deepen our compassion for ourselves – for our role in this world – and our compassion for ALL things that are part of making Earth the astonishing place she is. Perhaps it is as simple and profound as acknowledging the life force, the energy, that flows through all things.

And so...

The next few letters could take you to many places. Perhaps they will be among the ones you return to again and again; maybe you'll expand the practice and write to more beings; or maybe these EARTH letters will sit among the ones that are hardest to write.

Whatever arises is okay.

As you read the prompts that follow, the invitation is to let your words sink deep, to let them fly, to let them flow and to let them drift, saying whatever is waiting to be said. With love.

Dearest Mother Earth

I've found this letter so hard to write. There is such a well of sorrow in me – images of all your woundings flashing through me.

It feels almost impossible to see how I can write to you without getting lost in grief and guilt.

I'm asking my wisest guides to be with me as I write, to help me see that you already know all this. That you don't need me to lay out the troubles as a litany of woe. Because, my darling land stretches before me too.

The trees and grass and fields and flowers. There is so much green here. That sight fills my head and my heart until nothing else remains. I spoke to a friend and told her of the magic of this land, as though it is separate in some way from the whole of you.

But, of course, that isn't true.

Where there is scarring, still there is such intense beauty.

Where there is wild abundance, still there is pain.

This memory that's rising in me, as I write, of the unity of all things. How I am of you, of the stars that you are. How astonishing to know we are one.

And now, my opening words, dearest Mother Earth, are feeling even more true than I ever could have believed.

With love and sorrow and the most wondrous joy.

Dear One

The way you love this land, loves me. The way you see this land, sees me. The way you walk on this land is felt by me.

What you take from this land is given freely by me. What you give this land is received by me. When you first came to this land, I felt you walk into my arms and howl like the Wolf I know lives in you.

You stood under the stars and we fell in love, you and I – though I, of course, had always loved you, it was sweet to see you love me too. I know that out beyond this place your heart aches – so much it makes you avert your eyes and drag your gaze back to my hills and valley, which you've made your home.

Don't ignore the wounds, my love. Help tend them whatever way you can. I am all that I am. And you are all that you are. Made of the same star stuff, as you so rightly say. Perhaps between us we can find a way that lets you bathe in my beauty and bathe my wounds, so we can all heal again.

This may feel like a heavy burden and I don't say it to weigh you down – I tell you because the way you love the land stretched out before you is the way to hold the whole of me; the way that I hold the whole of you.

With love.

A letter of love to Earth

A letter of love from Earth

And so, as I listen to you all, it seems to me, a single song can be intensely beautiful, but it's all the songs together that creates the harmony.

A letter of love to Birds

Sweet River

Flowing force.
Gentle power.
Fierce spirit.
Freedom.

These are all how I see you.

Gathering place.
Cool balm.
Hope.
The endless flow.

Holding space for what
swims upstream; thoughts
and feelings pushing hard
against the current of release.

The joy of letting go.
Drifting with you.
Being you.
Reading you.
No beginning and no end
to how you wash through.
Surrendering.
Allowing.
Going with the slow.
Remembering you, and your
sisters – the sea, the stream,
the rain – your constancy through
times of love and pain. Beautiful
guide. I bring you my worries and
my fears and ask you to carry
them for me; out into the oceans,
releasing me of their weight, so
I can feel as free as you.

With love.

A letter of love to River

Big beautiful cloudy grey blueness

Looking into you at night blows my mind. It seems I simply haven't space within me to hold room for the thought of the space of you. But seeing you now, black shadows drifting on the edges, grey clouds sponged across a watery blue, I feel a sense of comfort.

Perhaps it's that you aren't there at night that makes things feel all too huge?

Where do you go?

Not the science of you, Sky, but the beingness of you?

Here you are, Earth's roof (can I describe you as that?) and then Sun goes down and you give way to Night with her billions of stars and billions of miles of travelling light.

I like you being here. It feels too small to say it that way, but it's so heartfelt. I like this feeling of waking and seeing how you colour the day.

I like seeing the tops of the trees feather your edges, your breath drifting among them, sometimes rising up as if the trees are breathing you.

Maybe they are.

I like it when you're brilliant and dazzling, when everything glitters, and I like it when you're heavy and wet and moisture hangs in the air like unspoken meaning.

I went through a phase of greeting you each day. I'm sorry I'd forgotten about that.

I'll start again.

With love.

A letter of love to Sky

Others

So much in our love of others can feel unsaid.

Maybe caught behind convention, lost in loyalty or hidden in the folds of other words.

And so, these letters feel particularly profound to me.

I recognize this is a reflection of my own conventions, loyalties and enfolding words but maybe they feel particularly profound for you too, in some way?

We all carry stories, memories, loves and losses. And whether our connection with someone is through blood or partnership or position or care-giving, the truth of our Self within that connection is ours to tell.

Maybe this is a time to speak of gratitude for all you have been given, to resolve something or perhaps to return an emotional burden you no longer wish to carry.

Sometimes, of course, painful memories can arise. Feelings of grief, regret, sorrow.

Intentionally holding all of these feelings in a bubble of kindness allows them to be present, AND helps us stay in the moment, without losing our way in their narrative.

This focus on kindness feels to me like a vital part of the ritual of writing Letters of Love.

And it's a beautiful way to hold space for the (virtual) recipient of your letter, particularly if forgiveness (yours or theirs) is playing a part.

So, call on your compassion if something complex or painful arises when you're writing.

For example, allowing yourself the option to pause, to reconnect with your ritual or your intention, can help you reground yourself, easing any painful thoughts or making them feel a little easier to hold.

A path here, if you're noticing something that needs some deeper care, is to journal about what's arising, or perhaps write a separate letter to that particular thought, feeling or sensation. This can be a wonderful way of gently exploring, with profound love, what is asking for your kindest attention.

As you write these letters to OTHERS, hold space for the whole of you; for your words, your meaning, your feelings, and your memories.

Whatever arises, go gently and write... with love.

I want to tell you that things are okay. We are okay. That I have survived hard things, that I still love fiercely, that I still laugh at the silliness of life. That I remember moments in your arms as a child that still make me smile. I want to tell you that I still think of you – and that I know you think of me still.

A letter of love to my mother

A letter of love to my father

Dearest G

I'm not sure I've ever told you of a piece of Work I once did.

Not work as you might think it – I mean, the inner stuff... the stuff we sometimes speak of.

At the time, I was invited to imagine the men that stood behind you – your father, grandfather and on through all the greats.

Seven generations in a line.

And as I looked along, and pictured their faces in my mind, I saw the sacrifice and effort they had given to ensure each next generation could survive.

And at once I understood the stories that they held, stories carried through our line of how to love and be loved in return.

And I was grateful for it all. It opened up a window I hadn't known was there. I'm amazed at how far we've come, you and I. Not just in geography and opportunity but able to speak at times of things that dig deep beneath the surface – like the miners you were born from – perhaps that's my legacy after all?

Maybe in truth none of us fall that far from the tree – but the gift we're given is to decide which way we wish to grow?

Thank you for letting me know it was okay to grow into me.

With love.

Dear Ones

So many of you gathered here.

How did this happen?

All this love that went with you to wherever it is you all now reside.

Though, did the love travel too?

Has it stayed here, with me?

It feels that way.

As I'm writing, I'm smiling to myself. I can feel you leaning over my shoulder, reading as I write. Knowing before I do what really needs to be said. You're all so wise now – at least that's how it seems to me. All those human frailties forgotten, dropped away with the bodies you left behind.

So you are, all of you, simply the stuff of true life, true love.

How wonderful that is. To know there's nothing that needs to be hidden, because you already know it all.

To know you are no longer separate, because you are all One.

To know I can reach you in any moment, because you are always here.

Gosh. I didn't know I knew so much; it makes me wonder who is writing now? You or me?

Thank you for loving me, and letting me love you. It feels such a blessing to have known you, even though, from this place, our time together has always seemed too short.

Until we meet again.

With love.

A letter of love to departed souls

Young Heart

This little letter is a loving reminder. A note to say we are all here. Every single one of us – we all hold you so dear.

And every time you think of us, you bring us close to you. We've been sending little messages – so wonderful that you see them.

Feathers and the dragonflies, the dancing butterflies and that scent that only you can sense – it's how we think of you.

With love.

A letter of love from departed souls

A letter of love and forgiveness

I wasn't sure who to write to here. There aren't many people I feel there is anything to forgive.

And then I thought of you. You'll see I didn't know how to address you – a term of endearment feels too hard right now, but let's see how we go.

So, how to forgive you?

A teacher once told me that forgiveness creates hierarchy – a magnanimity that implies an 'I'm better than you-ness'. And that led me to wonder whether truly the only person we can extend our forgiveness to is ourselves.

So, perhaps I'll begin there. I'll forgive myself for not seeing all that you were. And I'll love myself so fiercely through all that happened then, that nothing more can get through – a fire of love and light wrapped all around me; illuminating you in all your flawed humanity.

And there. There I can see my compassion spark. A flame in the dark. Lighting my way, so my true forgiveness of you can come through. Not in the hierarchical way my teacher spoke of but seeing you as someone who was, of course, limited by what they knew – and that is all any of us can ever know. I hope things changed for you. I hope you learned to forgive yourself too.

With love.

Emotions

We are feeling beings. Of course.

Our emotions express what runs beneath the surface of our tender skin.

They shape how we experience and respond to the world around us. They are part of us.

And they are worthy of our love... even those emotions we may wish we didn't have, or that we feel life could be easier without.

Making sense of our emotions, connecting with them, listening to them without being overwhelmed by them. For me this is one of the most wonderful aspects of the deep Inner Work that is available to us all.

But how?

A useful question, when our emotions feel heavy, complicated or highly activated, is to ask 'How is this serving me?'

Our immediate response might be 'It's not!' but when we look deeper, we can sometimes (often, always?) see it's trying to help us in some way. It can be enlightening.

It could be there's a part of us carrying an old protective strategy; an attempt to keep us safe in the world. Perhaps with another part, or parts, trying to stop us feeling that way: unhappy, frustrated, embarrassed or angry about how we're feeling. It can get complicated in there.

The renowned psychotherapist Viktor Frankl once wrote: 'Between stimulus and response there is a space. In that space is our power to choose our response. In our response lies our growth and our freedom.'

Creating some space within us, a space where we can see or feel the emotions as they arise, can be so useful in helping us choose our response – seeing what might serve us even more in the moment.

So, rather than judging ourselves harshly for what we're feeling, we learn to hold all our emotions gently. Remembering it's not the whole of us that feels that way – simply a part trying to do its best.

This reframe, this shift into greeting our emotions kindly, whatever they are, can feel uncomfortable at first. Particularly if we've been taught, or perhaps learned in the past, to suppress them, ignore them or shun them or fear them.

This can be BIG work, and so we go softly. These letters to EMOTIONS are an opportunity to listen in to what you'd really love them to know.

I've shared prompts for a handful of the emotions we all experience. The invitation is to extend this practice and see how it could support you to write to others too – all with love, of course.

And so, my loves, I am making space, holding space, and saying with my kindest voice: you too... you too are welcome here.

A letter of love to my fears

A letter of love to anger

Dearest black Dog,
fierce and loving Wolf

You have seemed as both to me, though now – in my Self – you seem wilder and more free.

No longer needing to stand beside and bark at all that moves in case it threatens me.

What a creature you are.

So much love, I now see, is what you have offered.

And I hope you see that love is now returned – though for many years you frightened me.

I was never sure how to hold you.

The sharp teeth you showed seemed to be bared at me – I see, now, of course, that you always had your back to me – or perhaps a truer word would be you had my back.

It's funny, when I think of the times I let you through, it was always with some righteous indignation at an act by some 'one' against an 'other' (it was okay to let you protect them); when some value of fairness or truth or loyalty felt impinged.

Then it was okay to unleash you… but never when it was my own pain or sadness you were angry about.

Then I had to keep you quiet. Stop you howling at the moon, in case you were heard, and I was thought unhappy.

Sweet hound that's grown into this wild creature of the woods.

How much love I have for you now. Such a relief to be able to hug you, dance with you.

To know you are always here, ready to stand by my side, for when I truly need you; ready to be asked but not imposing.

This feels like the kindest gift of all. The most generous offering of protection.

And I receive it.

With love.

A letter of love to sadness

Soft Sadness

I wasn't sure how to begin this message to you.

I want to tell you how much I love you, how you don't need to hide away, how there is nothing about you I am ashamed of (though I know it didn't always seem that way).

I want to tell you, you have a place, that you are just as vital as my joy and anger and my pain. I want to tell you it's all okay.

Even when it's not, it is all okay.

I want to tell you that again and again and again and I want to hold you in my arms – not only when you're weeping but when you're quietly reflecting too.

I want to wrap you up in all that's safe and warm, and let you know we can weather every storm. And that it's okay to feel just as you do.

There's room within me, for the depth and breadth of you.

With love,

PS: It seems I did know how to begin, after all.

My precious Joy

Oh! Spring-like essence! Effervescence! Just writing your name is joyful. Joy FULL!

The light and lightness I feel when I am with you. You have been my companion and my dearest friend.

There have been many times when I thought I had lost you. When I thought you had wandered in my grief, when I thought the seriousness of my life had crushed you too – but you always returned.

Most loving friend. A tiny spark of light that grew and grew until I knew it was you.

And I could breathe again.

With love.

A letter of love to joy

Tender Hope and Dreams

There was a time, Hope, when I felt you'd departed. Or rather I shunned you as 'that bitter disappointment I once called hope'.

Sorry about that.

It feels a little dramatic and unkind now – though things were feeling rather tough at the time.

I didn't understand then that you're not the thing I was clinging to.

Now I see you are the essence of my heart's Dreams. And that out of you comes everything.

It's feeling a little messy to explain – though of course, you know what you are.

I think what I'm trying to say in this letter is that now I understand that what we wanted at the time was something different to what came about.

And that is okay.

That is SO okay.

This is where we are meant to be and I am so grateful for that. Though, as I say, at the time it felt hard to believe something was what was meant to be and then learn it was meant to be something else.

I'm sorry, it feels like I'm waffling but this is hard to write to you.

And maybe that's the heart of it?

My relationship with you has always somehow been better when it's been floating in the grey. When I haven't grabbed or grasped at some part of you, but let you coalesce into whatever you (somehow) knew was right for me.

This feels like such an important learning.

Thank you for bearing with me as I found my way.

With love.

A letter of love to my hopes and dreams

A letter of love to LOVE

A letter of love from LOVE

Each Inner Workbook is a personal guide for deep self-reflection. Dive into your thoughts, emotions and experiences – and connect to the wisdom, compassion and fire within.

If you sense it is time to heal old wounds, let go of holding yourself back or step into a new chapter in your life, these guided journals have been created to help you explore and find your way.

- Embrace change, even when you're uncertain.
- Feel at ease with who you are.
- Live on purpose and follow your passions.
- Courageously bring your inner dreams to life.

Discover yourself at
www.innerworkproject.com

If you're curious to experience more Flow Journaling, see *In the Flow: Journal your inner wisdom*. Part workbook, part guide, it's full of useful insights and compassion-based journaling prompts.

And if you are searching for direction, see *On Purpose: Discover the meaning of your life.* This is a treasure map for self-discovery, guiding you through a transformative journey of finding your gifts and living a purposeful life.

To remember and explore the meaning of your dreams and how they connect with your waking life, see *Dreamwork: Unlock the secrets of your dreams*. Become your own dream interpreter and begin to co-create with your dreams.

And to practise the art of creating and using affirmations, see *I Am: A month of affirmations for inner peace and joy*. Learn to let go of the old stories you hold about yourself and open up to new possibilities.

About Henny Flynn

Henny lives in Herefordshire, England, with her husband and their dog, Ronnie.

She writes, coaches, speaks and teaches about making and managing deep and lasting change with profound compassion.

You can Journal with Henny through her online gatherings and in-person retreats. Connect with her at hennyflynn.co.uk and hear her on the Henny Flynn podcast.

Information:

First published:
Inner Work Project, 2025

Text copyright ©
Henny Flynn 2025

All rights reserved.
ISBN 978-1-916563-06-3

Graphic Design:
Supafrank

Printed in the UK by Pureprint.

Discover more workbooks to put your good intentions into daily practice.

www.innerworkproject.com